#1 SISTER

SISTER

summersdale

FOR THE BEST SISTER EVER

An Hachette UK Company
www.hachette.co.uk

Summersdale Publishers Ltd
Part of Octopus Publishing Group Limited
Carmelite House
50 Victoria Embankment
LONDON
EC4Y 0DZ

www.summersdale.com

Printed and bound in China

ISBN: 978-1-78685-992-1

Substantial discounts on bulk quantities of Summersdale books are available to corporations, professional associations and other organizations. For details contact general enquiries: telephone: +44 (0) 1243 771107 or email: enquiries@summersdale.com.

TO..*Diana*..............

FROM.*Sheryl*.......

IS SOLACE ANYWHERE MORE
COMFORTING THAN THAT IN
THE ARMS OF A SISTER?

Alice Walker

"

WHATEVER YOU DO THEY WILL LOVE YOU.

Deborah Moggach

"

THE BOND
THAT LINKS
YOUR TRUE
FAMILY IS
NOT ONE OF
BLOOD, BUT OF
RESPECT AND
JOY IN EACH
OTHER'S LIFE.

RICHARD BACH

YOU CAN KID
THE WORLD, BUT
NOT YOUR
SISTER.

CHARLOTTE GRAY

FRIENDS

MAY COME

AND GO, BUT

SISTERS ARE

FOREVER

I SUSTAIN MYSELF
WITH THE LOVE
OF FAMILY.

MAYA ANGELOU

ALL WOMEN ARE NATURALLY BADASS.

Alicia Keys

> A FAMILY IS A UNIT COMPOSED NOT ONLY OF CHILDREN BUT OF MEN, WOMEN, AN OCCASIONAL ANIMAL, AND THE COMMON COLD.

Ogden Nash

HELPING ONE ANOTHER IS PART OF THE RELIGION OF OUR SISTERHOOD.

LOUISA MAY ALCOTT

I HAVE A SISTER,
I KNOW I
ALWAYS HAVE

A FRIEND

ARE WE NOT LIKE TWO
VOLUMES OF ONE BOOK?

Marceline Desbordes-Valmore

FOLLOW YOUR OWN STAR.

DANTE ALIGHIERI

IN THEE MY SOUL SHALL
HOLD COMBINED
THE SISTER AND THE FRIEND.

Catherine Killigrew

> BROTHERS AND SISTERS ARE AS CLOSE AS HANDS AND FEET.

Vietnamese proverb

A HAPPY FAMILY IS BUT AN EARLIER HEAVEN.

GEORGE BERNARD SHAW

CHILDREN OF THE SAME FAMILY,
THE SAME BLOOD, WITH THE
SAME FIRST ASSOCIATIONS AND
HABITS, HAVE SOME MEANS
OF ENJOYMENT IN THEIR
POWER, WHICH NO SUBSEQUENT
CONNECTIONS CAN SUPPLY.

Jane Austen

"

THERE IS NO LIMIT
TO WHAT WE,
AS WOMEN, CAN
ACCOMPLISH.

Michelle Obama

"

REJOICE WITH YOUR FAMILY IN THE BEAUTIFUL LAND OF LIFE!

ALBERT EINSTEIN

SISTER IS PROBABLY THE MOST
COMPETITIVE RELATIONSHIP
WITHIN THE FAMILY, BUT
ONCE THE SISTERS ARE
GROWN, IT BECOMES THE
STRONGEST RELATIONSHIP.

Margaret Mead

YOU BRING

OUT MY

INNER CHILD

BLESS YOU, MY DARLING, AND REMEMBER YOU ARE ALWAYS IN THE HEART... OF YOUR SISTER.

KATHERINE MANSFIELD

A SISTER CAN BE SEEN AS
SOMEONE WHO IS BOTH
OURSELVES AND VERY MUCH
NOT OURSELVES — A SPECIAL
KIND OF DOUBLE.

Toni Morrison

"

YOU DON'T CHOOSE YOUR FAMILY. THEY ARE GOD'S GIFT TO YOU, AS YOU ARE TO THEM.

Desmond Tutu

OTHER THINGS MAY
CHANGE US, BUT WE
START AND END
WITH FAMILY.

Anthony Brandt

MORE THAN
SANTA CLAUS, YOUR
SISTER KNOWS WHEN
YOU'VE BEEN BAD
AND GOOD.

LINDA SUNSHINE

OUR ROOTS

SAY WE'RE SISTERS,
OUR HEARTS SAY
WE'RE FRIENDS

SISTERLY LOVE IS, OF ALL SENTIMENTS, THE MOST ABSTRACT.

UGO BETTI

EVERY FAMILY HAS A STORY THAT IT TELLS ITSELF, THAT IT PASSES ON TO THE CHILDREN AND GRANDCHILDREN. THE STORY GROWS OVER THE YEARS... IT BECOMES THE FLAGPOLE THAT THE FAMILY HANGS ITS IDENTITY FROM.

A. M. Homes

“

NO ONE CAN MAKE YOU FEEL INFERIOR WITHOUT YOUR CONSENT.

Eleanor Roosevelt

”

FAMILY IS WHAT GROUNDS YOU.

ANGELINA JOLIE

THERE CAN BE NO SITUATION
IN LIFE IN WHICH THE
CONVERSATION OF MY DEAR
SISTER WILL NOT ADMINISTER
SOME COMFORT TO ME.

Mary Wortley Montagu

WHEN SISTERS STAND SHOULDER TO SHOULDER, WHO STANDS A CHANCE AGAINST US?

PAM BROWN

YOU CAN KISS YOUR FAMILY
AND FRIENDS GOODBYE AND PUT
MILES BETWEEN YOU, BUT AT THE
SAME TIME YOU CARRY THEM
WITH YOU IN YOUR HEART.

Frederick Buechner

YOU ALWAYS KNOW THE RIGHT THING TO SAY, EVEN IF IT'S NOT WHAT I WANT TO HEAR!

A SISTER IS BOTH
YOUR MIRROR –
AND YOUR OPPOSITE.

Elizabeth Fishel

"

MOST ARE
LIKE MY SISTER
AND ME... LINKED BY
VOLATILE LOVE, BEST
FRIENDS WHO MAKE
OTHER BEST FRIENDS
EVER SO SLIGHTLY
LESS BEST.

Patricia Volk

"

I, WHO HAVE
NO SISTERS
OR BROTHERS,
LOOK WITH
SOME DEGREE
OF INNOCENT
ENVY ON THOSE
WHO MAY BE
SAID TO BE BORN
TO FRIENDS.

JAMES BOSWELL

THE FAMILY –
THAT DEAR
OCTOPUS FROM
WHOSE TENTACLES
WE NEVER QUITE
ESCAPE, NOR, IN
OUR INMOST HEARTS,
EVER QUITE WISH TO.

DODIE SMITH

A SISTER

IS A
FOREVER
FRIEND

SISTERS FUNCTION AS
SAFETY NETS IN A CHAOTIC
WORLD SIMPLY BY BEING
THERE FOR EACH OTHER.

Carol Saline

"

SWEET IS THE VOICE
OF A SISTER IN THE
SEASON OF SORROW,
AND WISE IS THE
COUNSEL OF THOSE
WHO LOVE US.

Benjamin Disraeli

"

BEING YOURSELF
AND BEING TRUE TO
WHAT MAKES YOU
HAPPY IS THE MOST
IMPORTANT
THING.

ZOOEY DESCHANEL

BECAUSE THERE'S ONE
THING STRONGER THAN
MAGIC: SISTERHOOD.

Robin Benway

IF YOU LOOK DEEPLY
INTO THE PALM OF
YOUR HAND, YOU
WILL SEE YOUR
PARENTS AND ALL
GENERATIONS OF
YOUR ANCESTORS.
ALL OF THEM ARE
ALIVE IN THIS
MOMENT. EACH
IS PRESENT IN
YOUR BODY.

THÍCH NHẤT HẠNH

A SISTER

SHARES

CHILDHOOD

MEMORIES AND

GROWN-UP

DREAMS

THE FAMILY IS
THE COUNTRY
OF THE HEART.

Giuseppe Mazzini

> YOU KNOW FULL WELL AS I DO THE VALUE OF SISTERS' AFFECTIONS: THERE IS NOTHING LIKE IT IN THIS WORLD.

Charlotte Brontë

IN TIME OF TEST,
FAMILY IS BEST.

Burmese proverb

THERE IS NO
BETTER FRIEND
THAN A SISTER.
AND THERE IS NO
BETTER SISTER
THAN YOU.

ANONYMOUS

HAVING

A SISTER MEANS
ALWAYS HAVING
 BACKUP

FOLLOW YOUR INNER MOONLIGHT; DON'T HIDE THE MADNESS.

ALLEN GINSBERG

I DON'T BELIEVE AN ACCIDENT OF BIRTH MAKES PEOPLE SISTERS OR BROTHERS. SISTERHOOD AND BROTHERHOOD IS A CONDITION PEOPLE HAVE TO WORK AT.

Maya Angelou

" WOMEN SPEAKING UP FOR THEMSELVES AND FOR THOSE AROUND THEM IS THE STRONGEST FORCE WE HAVE TO CHANGE THE WORLD. "

Melinda Gates

FAMILY
COMES FIRST.
YOU'RE THE ONLY
THING THEY HAVE.

HEIDI KLUM

SOMEONE

TO LEAN ON,

SOMEONE TO

COUNT ON...

SOMEONE TO

TELL ON!

A SISTER SMILES WHEN ONE TELLS ONE'S STORIES — FOR SHE KNOWS WHERE THE DECORATION HAS BEEN ADDED.

Chris Montaigne

BE
UNAPOLOGETICALLY
YOU.

Steve Maraboli

SISTERHOOD IS POWERFUL.

ROBIN MORGAN

SISTER IS OUR FIRST FRIEND AND SECOND MOTHER.

Sunny Gupta

"

SISTERS ARE
THERE WITH US
FROM THE DAWN
OF OUR PERSONAL
STORIES TO THE
INEVITABLE DUSK.

Susan Scarf Merrell

"

YOU'RE

ALWAYS THERE
WHEN I NEED

WE ACQUIRE
FRIENDS AND WE
MAKE ENEMIES,
BUT OUR SISTERS
COME WITH THE
TERRITORY.

EVELYN LOEB

YOU KEEP YOUR PAST BY HAVING
SISTERS... THEY'RE THE ONLY
ONES WHO DON'T GET BORED IF
YOU TALK ABOUT YOUR MEMORIES.

Deborah Moggach

WE MAY LOOK OLD AND WISE TO THE OUTSIDE WORLD. BUT TO EACH OTHER, WE ARE STILL IN JUNIOR SCHOOL.

CHARLOTTE GRAY

FAMILY LIFE IS
TOO INTIMATE TO BE
PRESERVED BY THE
SPIRIT OF JUSTICE. IT
CAN BE SUSTAINED BY
A SPIRIT OF LOVE.

REINHOLD NIEBUHR

YOU ARE

THE BEST!

"SOMEONE WHO SEES YOU EXACTLY AS YOU ARE, AND THINKS THAT IS ENOUGH."

Barbara Bush on her sister

NEVER DOUBT THAT YOU ARE
VALUABLE AND POWERFUL AND
DESERVING OF EVERY CHANCE AND
OPPORTUNITY IN THE WORLD.

Hillary Clinton

WE HAVE BEEN BANDED
TOGETHER UNDER PACK CODES
AND TRIBAL LAWS.

Rose Macaulay

FOR THERE IS NO FRIEND LIKE A SISTER, IN CALM OR STORMY WEATHER.

CHRISTINA ROSSETTI

IN THE

COOKIES OF LIFE,

SISTERS

ARE THE
CHOCOLATE CHIPS

WHAT SETS SISTERS APART
FROM BROTHERS AND ALSO
FROM FRIENDS IS A VERY
INTIMATE MESHING OF HEART,
SOUL AND THE MYSTICAL
CORDS OF MEMORY.

Carol Saline

FAMILIES ARE THE COMPASS THAT GUIDE US.

BRAD HENRY

EVERY WOMAN
HAS THE RIGHT TO
BECOME HERSELF,
AND DO WHATEVER
SHE NEEDS TO DO.

Ani DiFranco

OUR SISTERS HOLD UP OUR MIRRORS: OUR IMAGES OF WHO WE ARE AND WHO WE CAN DARE TO BECOME.

ELIZABETH FISHEL

OUR DAYS OUT

TOGETHER

ARE THE

MOST FUN!

AN OLDER SISTER IS A FRIEND
AND DEFENDER — A LISTENER,
CONSPIRATOR, A COUNSELLOR
AND A SHARER OF DELIGHTS.
AND SORROWS TOO.

Pam Brown

IF WE ARE UNITED, THERE IS NO LIMIT TO WHAT WE CAN DO.

AMAL CLOONEY

OH... THE INEXPRESSIBLE
COMFORT OF FEELING SAFE WITH
A PERSON; HAVING NEITHER TO
WEIGH THOUGHTS NOR MEASURE
WORDS, BUT TO POUR THEM
ALL OUT, JUST AS THEY ARE.

Dinah Maria Craik

YOU HAVE TO BE UNIQUE, AND DIFFERENT, AND SHINE IN YOUR OWN WAY.

Lady Gaga

YOU

HELP ME

KNOW

WHO I REALLY AM

THERE IS SPACE WITHIN SISTERHOOD FOR LIKENESS AND DIFFERENCE, FOR THE SUBTLE DIFFERENCES THAT CHALLENGE AND DELIGHT... AND SURPRISE.

CHRISTINE DOWNING

SO WE GREW TOGETHER,
LIKE TO A DOUBLE CHERRY,
SEEMING PARTED,
BUT YET AN UNION IN PARTITION;
TWO LOVELY BERRIES MOULDED
ON ONE STEM.

William Shakespeare

FAMILY
COMES FIRST
FOR ME IN EVERY
SINGLE WAY.

JOHN KRASINSKI

"SISTERHOOD... IS, LIKE MOTHERHOOD, A CAPACITY, NOT A DESTINY. IT MUST BE CHOSEN, EXERCISED BY ACTS OF WILL.

Olga Broumas

A SISTER

WILL ALWAYS

UNDERSTAND

YOU ARE VALUED,
YOU ARE A GODDESS
AND DON'T FORGET THAT.

Jennifer Lopez

MAY YOU LIVE EVERY DAY OF YOUR LIFE.

JONATHAN SWIFT

THE LOVE OF FAMILY AND THE ADMIRATION OF FRIENDS IS MUCH MORE IMPORTANT THAN WEALTH AND PRIVILEGE.

CHARLES KURALT

THE FAMILY IS OUR REFUGE
AND OUR SPRINGBOARD;
NOURISHED ON IT, WE CAN
ADVANCE TO NEW HORIZONS.

Alex Haley

A TRUE SISTER

IS A FRIEND
WHO LISTENS
WITH HER

HEART

"

BE YOURSELF.
DO WHATEVER
YOU WANT TO DO
AND DON'T LET
BOUNDARIES
HOLD YOU BACK.

Sophie Turner

"

MY SISTER ACCOMMODATES ME...
SHE ACCEPTS AND LOVES ME,
DESPITE OUR DIFFERENCES.

Joy Harjo

MY FIRST JOB IS BIG SISTER AND I TAKE THAT VERY SERIOUSLY.

VENUS WILLIAMS

AN OUNCE OF BLOOD IS
WORTH MORE THAN A POUND
OF FRIENDSHIP.

Spanish proverb

IF I COULD CHOOSE MY FAMILY, I'D STILL CHOOSE YOU

FAMILY: LIKE BRANCHES
ON A TREE, WE ALL GROW IN
DIFFERENT DIRECTIONS, YET
OUR ROOTS REMAIN AS ONE.

Anonymous

"

MY SIBLINGS
ARE MY BEST
FRIENDS.

America Ferrera

"

BIG SISTERS ARE THE CRAB GRASS IN THE LAWN OF LIFE.

CHARLES M. SCHULZ

A FAMILY NEEDS TO WORK AS A TEAM, SUPPORTING EACH OTHER'S INDIVIDUAL AIMS AND ASPIRATIONS.

BUZZ ALDRIN

SHE'S MY LITTLE SISTER.
MINE TO TORTURE AND
MINE TO PROTECT.

Julia Quinn

SiSTER

TO SISTER WE
WILL ALWAYS BE,
A COUPLE OF NUTS
OFF THE FAMILY
 TREE

A MINISTERING ANGEL SHALL MY SISTER BE.

WILLIAM SHAKESPEARE

A GIRL SHOULD BE TWO THINGS: WHO AND WHAT SHE WANTS.

Coco Chanel

THE FAMILY IS ONE OF NATURE'S MASTERPIECES.

GEORGE SANTAYANA

JUST BE YOURSELF,

THERE IS NO ONE BETTER.

Taylor Swift

ONE REFUSING A SIBLING'S
ADVICE BREAKS HIS ARM.

Somali proverb

I KNOW OUR

FIGHTS WILL

NEVER LAST

YOUR PARENTS LEAVE YOU TOO
SOON AND YOUR KIDS AND
SPOUSE COME ALONG LATE, BUT
YOUR SIBLINGS KNOW YOU
WHEN YOU ARE IN YOUR MOST
INCHOATE FORM.

Jeffrey Kluger

"

TO US, FAMILY
MEANS PUTTING
YOUR ARMS AROUND
EACH OTHER AND
BEING THERE.

Barbara Bush

"

WE HAVE TO DARE TO BE OURSELVES, HOWEVER FRIGHTENING OR STRANGE THAT SELF MAY PROVE TO BE.

MAY SARTON

A FAMILY IN
HARMONY WILL
PROSPER IN
EVERYTHING.

CHINESE PROVERB

THERE IS NO DOUBT THAT IT IS AROUND THE FAMILY AND THE HOME THAT ALL THE GREATEST VIRTUES... ARE CREATED, STRENGTHENED AND MAINTAINED.

Winston Churchill

I'M SMILING

BECAUSE YOU'RE
MY SISTER. I'M
LAUGHING
BECAUSE THERE'S
NOTHING YOU CAN
DO ABOUT IT!

FAMILIES ARE
THE BEST PLACE
TO LEARN AND
PRACTISE MUTUAL
TOLERANCE AND
ACCEPTANCE.

BEGUM AGA KHAN

"

SIBLINGS: CHILDREN OF THE SAME PARENTS, EACH OF WHOM IS PERFECTLY NORMAL UNTIL THEY GET TOGETHER.

Sam Levenson

"

THE ONLY ROCK I KNOW THAT STAYS STEADY, THE ONLY INSTITUTION I KNOW THAT WORKS, IS THE FAMILY.

LEE IACOCCA

FAMILY FACES ARE MAGIC MIRRORS. LOOKING AT PEOPLE WHO BELONG TO US, WE SEE THE PAST, PRESENT, AND FUTURE.

Gail Lumet Buckley

YOU'RE BEAUTIFUL
AND WORTHY AND
TOTALLY UNIQUE.

Emma Stone

SISTERS ARE

FOR SHARING

LAUGHTER AND

WIPING TEARS

THERE IS GREAT COMFORT
AND INSPIRATION IN THE
FEELING OF CLOSE HUMAN
RELATIONSHIPS.

Walt Disney

"

YOU ARE PERFECTLY CAST IN YOUR LIFE. I CAN'T IMAGINE ANYONE BUT YOU IN THE ROLE. GO PLAY.

Lin-Manuel Miranda

"

A YOUNG LADY'S MOST NATURAL ALLY IS HER SISTER.

ANNA GODBERSEN

FAMILY IS NOT AN
IMPORTANT THING.
IT'S EVERYTHING.

MICHAEL J. FOX

OUR SIBLINGS... RESEMBLE US
JUST ENOUGH TO MAKE ALL THEIR
DIFFERENCES CONFUSING...
WE ARE CAST IN RELATION TO
THEM OUR WHOLE LIVES LONG.

Susan Scarf Merrell

YOU'RE

MY BEST

FRIEND

NEVER BEND
YOUR HEAD.
ALWAYS HOLD IT
HIGH. LOOK THE
WORLD STRAIGHT
IN THE EYE.

HELEN KELLER

> "WE CANNOT DESTROY KINDRED: OUR CHAINS STRETCH A LITTLE SOMETIMES, BUT THEY NEVER BREAK."
>
> Marquise de Sévigné

TO EACH OTHER, WE WERE AS NORMAL AND NICE AS THE SMELL OF BREAD. WE WERE JUST A FAMILY.

JOHN IRVING

YOU CAN BE BORING AND
TEDIOUS WITH SISTERS,
WHEREAS YOU HAVE TO PUT ON
A GOOD FACE WITH FRIENDS.

Deborah Moggach

YOU KNOW

JUST HOW

TO MAKE

ME SMILE

FAMILIES... HUMANIZE YOU.
THEY ARE MADE TO MAKE
YOU FORGET YOURSELF
OCCASIONALLY, SO THAT THE
BEAUTIFUL BALANCE OF LIFE
IS NOT DESTROYED.

Anaïs Nin

HOW GOOD IT IS
TO HAVE A SISTER
WHOSE HEART IS
AS YOUNG AS
YOUR OWN.

Pam Brown

THE INFORMALITY OF FAMILY
LIFE IS A BLESSED CONDITION
THAT ALLOWS US ALL TO BECOME
OUR BEST WHILE LOOKING
OUR WORST.

Marge Kennedy

DON'T YOU EVER LET
A SOUL IN THE WORLD
TELL YOU THAT YOU
CAN'T BE EXACTLY
WHO YOU ARE.

LADY GAGA

I KNOW

I CAN SHARE
ANYTHING WITH

IN FAMILY LIFE, LOVE IS THE OIL THAT EASES FRICTION, THE CEMENT THAT BINDS... AND THE MUSIC THAT BRINGS HARMONY.

EVA BURROWS

FAMILY LIFE... ETCHES
ITSELF INTO MEMORY AND
PERSONALITY. IT'S DIFFICULT
TO IMAGINE ANYTHING MORE
NOURISHING TO THE SOUL.

Thomas Moore

> **MY SISTER TAUGHT ME EVERYTHING I REALLY NEED TO KNOW, AND SHE WAS ONLY IN SIXTH GRADE AT THE TIME.**
>
> Linda Sunshine

BE YOURSELF.
THE WORLD
WORSHIPS
THE ORIGINAL.

INGRID BERGMAN

ALWAYS REMEMBER, YOU HAVE
WITHIN YOU THE STRENGTH, THE
PATIENCE, AND THE PASSION
TO REACH FOR THE STARS,
TO CHANGE THE WORLD.

Harriet Tubman

FAMILY IS THE MOST IMPORTANT THING IN THE WORLD.

DIANA, PRINCESS OF WALES

SISTERS ARE DIFFERENT FLOWERS FROM THE SAME GARDEN

A SISTER IS ONE OF THE
NICEST THINGS THAT CAN
HAPPEN TO ANYONE.

Anonymous

RIDE THE ENERGY
OF YOUR OWN
UNIQUE SPIRIT.

Gabrielle Roth

SIBLING RELATIONSHIPS...
FLOURISH IN A THOUSAND
INCARNATIONS OF CLOSENESS
AND DISTANCE, WARMTH,
LOYALTY AND DISTRUST.

Erica E. Goode

NOTHING CAN
DIM THE LIGHT
WHICH SHINES
FROM WITHIN.

MAYA ANGELOU

THERE IS NO TIME LIKE THE OLD TIME, WHEN YOU AND I WERE YOUNG!

OLIVER WENDELL HOLMES

YOU ARE MAGNIFICENT
BEYOND MEASURE, PERFECT
IN YOUR IMPERFECTIONS,
AND WONDERFULLY MADE.

Abiola Abrams

KEEP YOUR EYES ON THE STARS, BUT REMEMBER TO KEEP YOUR FEET ON THE GROUND.

THEODORE ROOSEVELT

YOU KNOW

ALL MY SECRETS –
AND STILL

LOVE ME!

" WHAT GREATER THING IS THERE FOR TWO HUMAN SOULS THAN TO FEEL THAT THEY ARE JOINED FOR LIFE... TO BE ONE WITH EACH OTHER IN SILENT UNSPEAKABLE MEMORIES.

George Eliot

"

DON'T LET THEM TAME YOU.

ISADORA DUNCAN

THERE IS AN
INTERCONNECTEDNESS
AMONG MEMBERS THAT
BONDS THE FAMILY, MUCH
LIKE MOUNTAIN CLIMBERS
WHO ROPE THEMSELVES
TOGETHER WHEN CLIMBING.

Phil McGraw

> THE STRENGTH OF A FAMILY, LIKE THE STRENGTH OF AN ARMY, LIES IN ITS LOYALTY TO EACH OTHER.

Mario Puzo

WHEN YOU LOOK AT YOUR LIFE,
THE GREATEST HAPPINESSES ARE
FAMILY HAPPINESSES.

Joyce Brothers

If you're interested in finding out more about our books, find us on Facebook at **Summersdale Publishers** and follow us on Twitter at **@Summersdale**.

www.summersdale.com